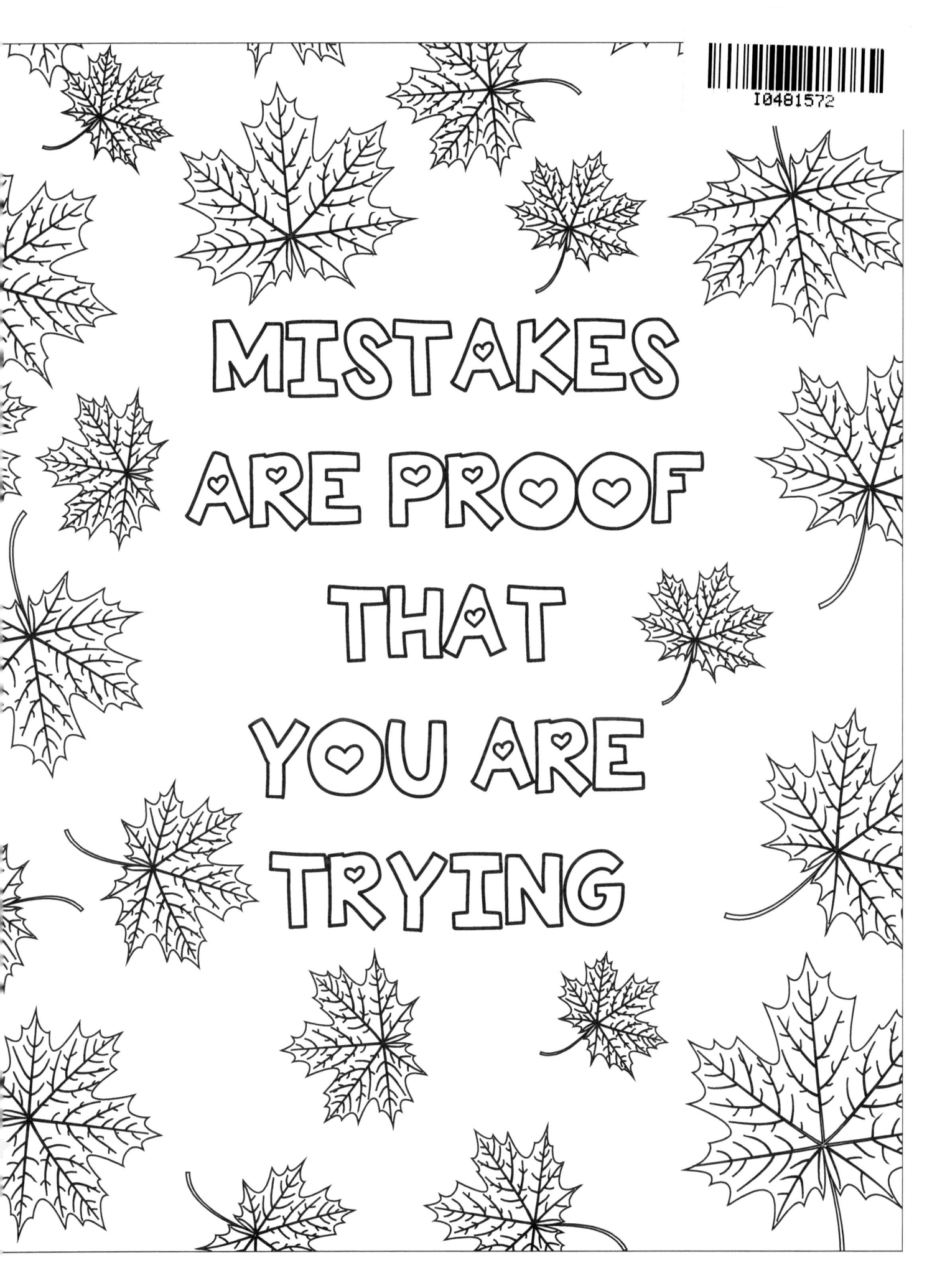

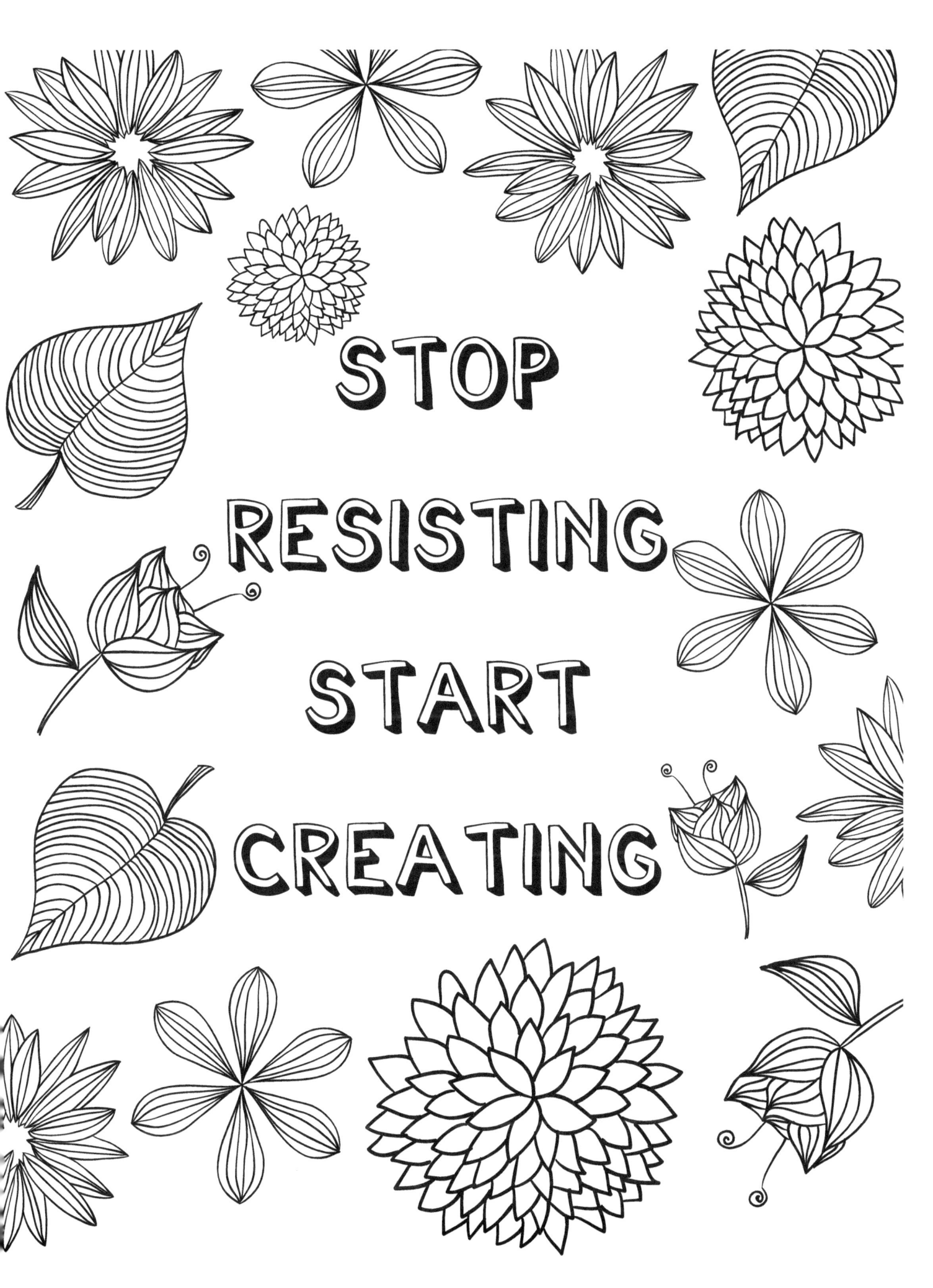

STOP RESISTING START CREATING

BE STRONG AND KICK ASS

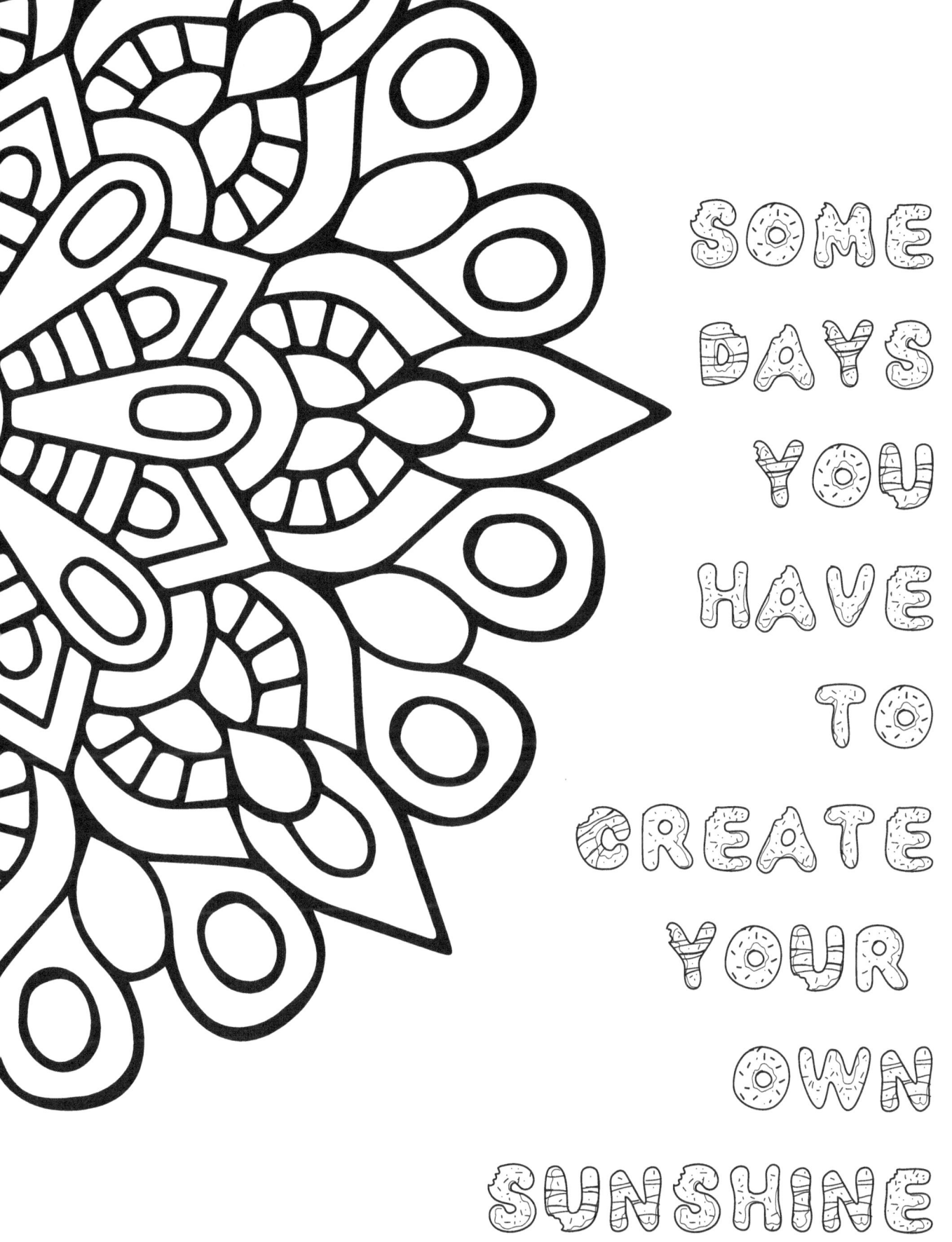

SOME DAYS YOU HAVE TO CREATE YOUR OWN SUNSHINE

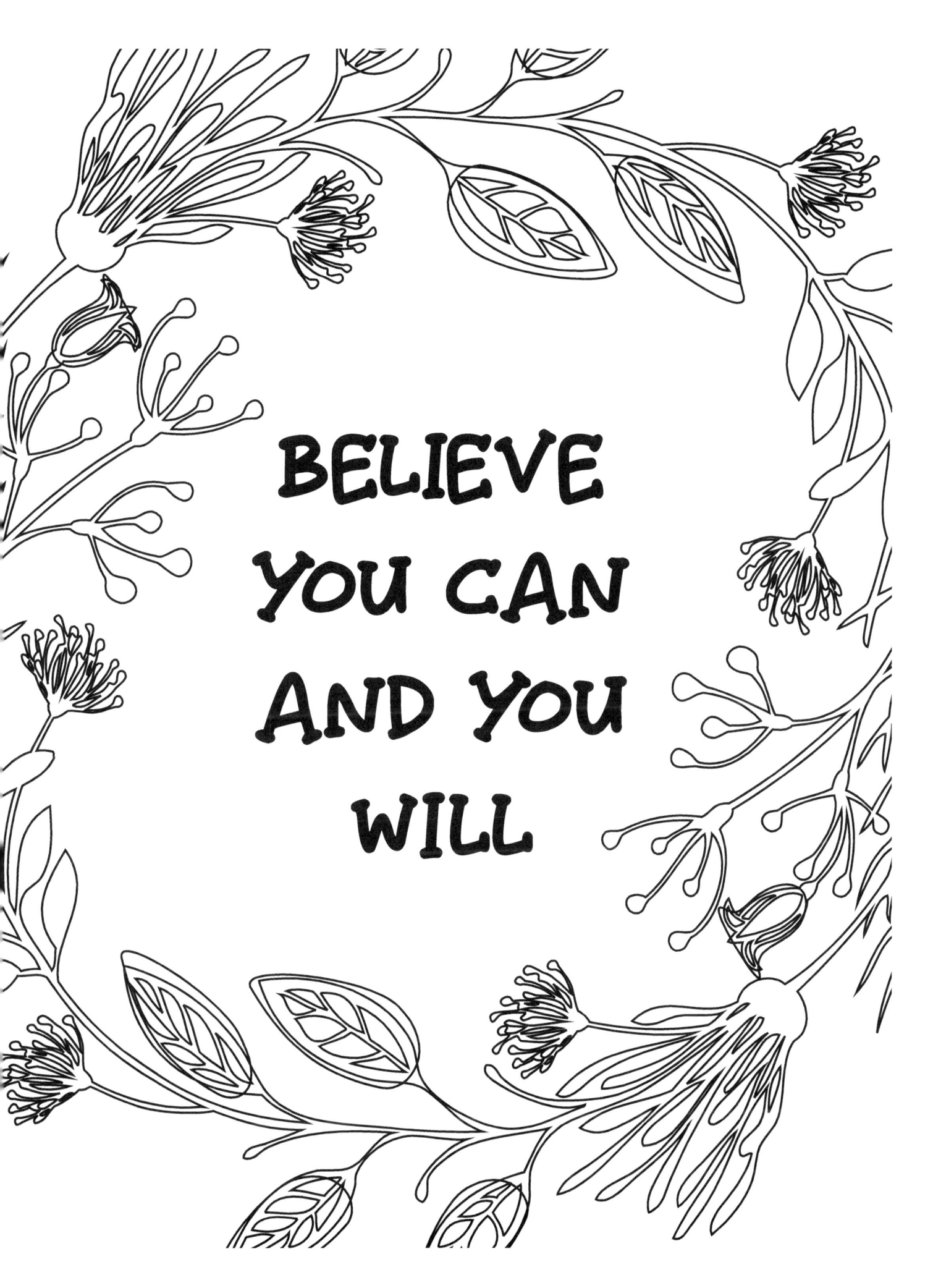

DO YOUR BEST AND FORGET THE REST

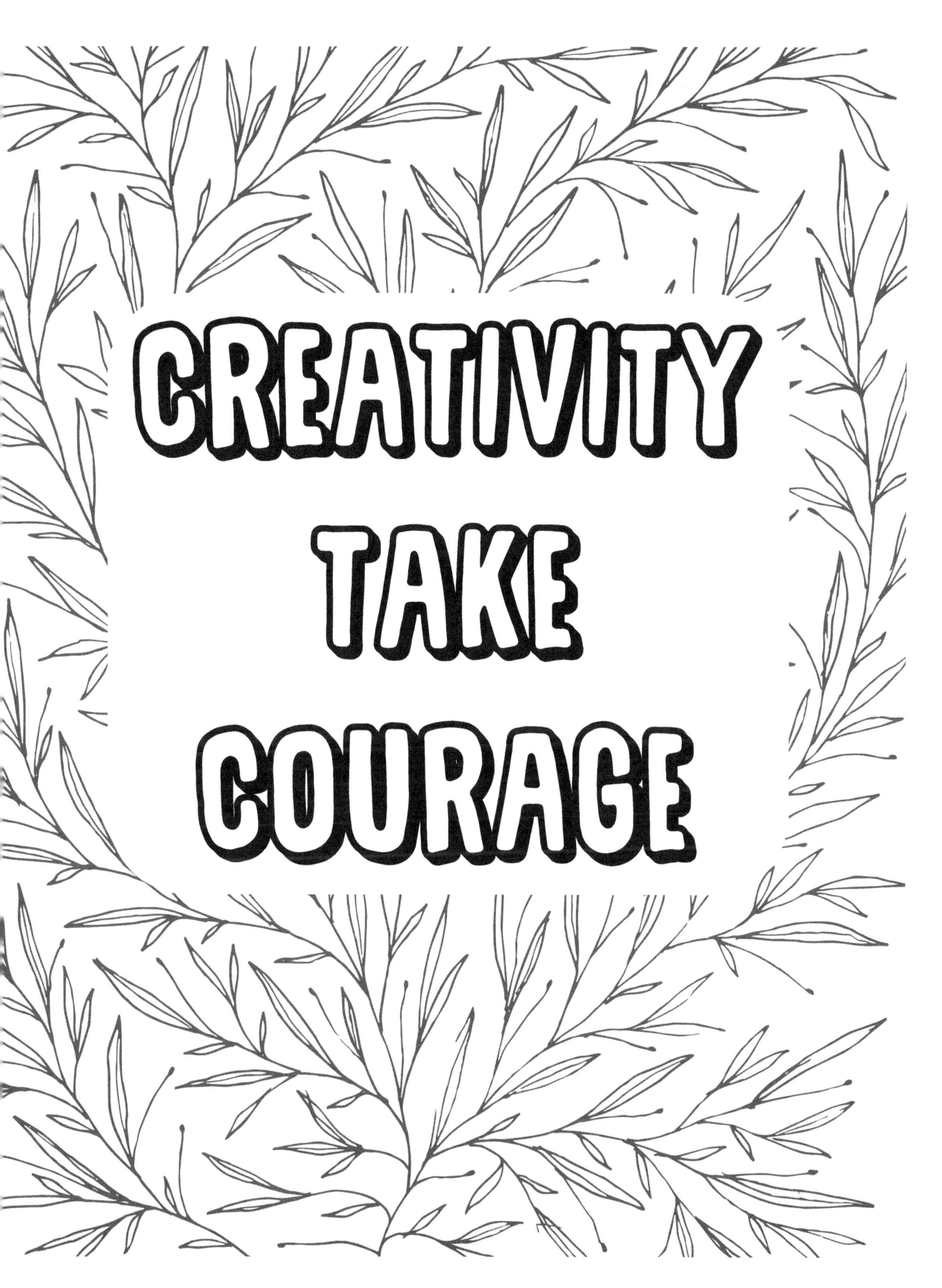

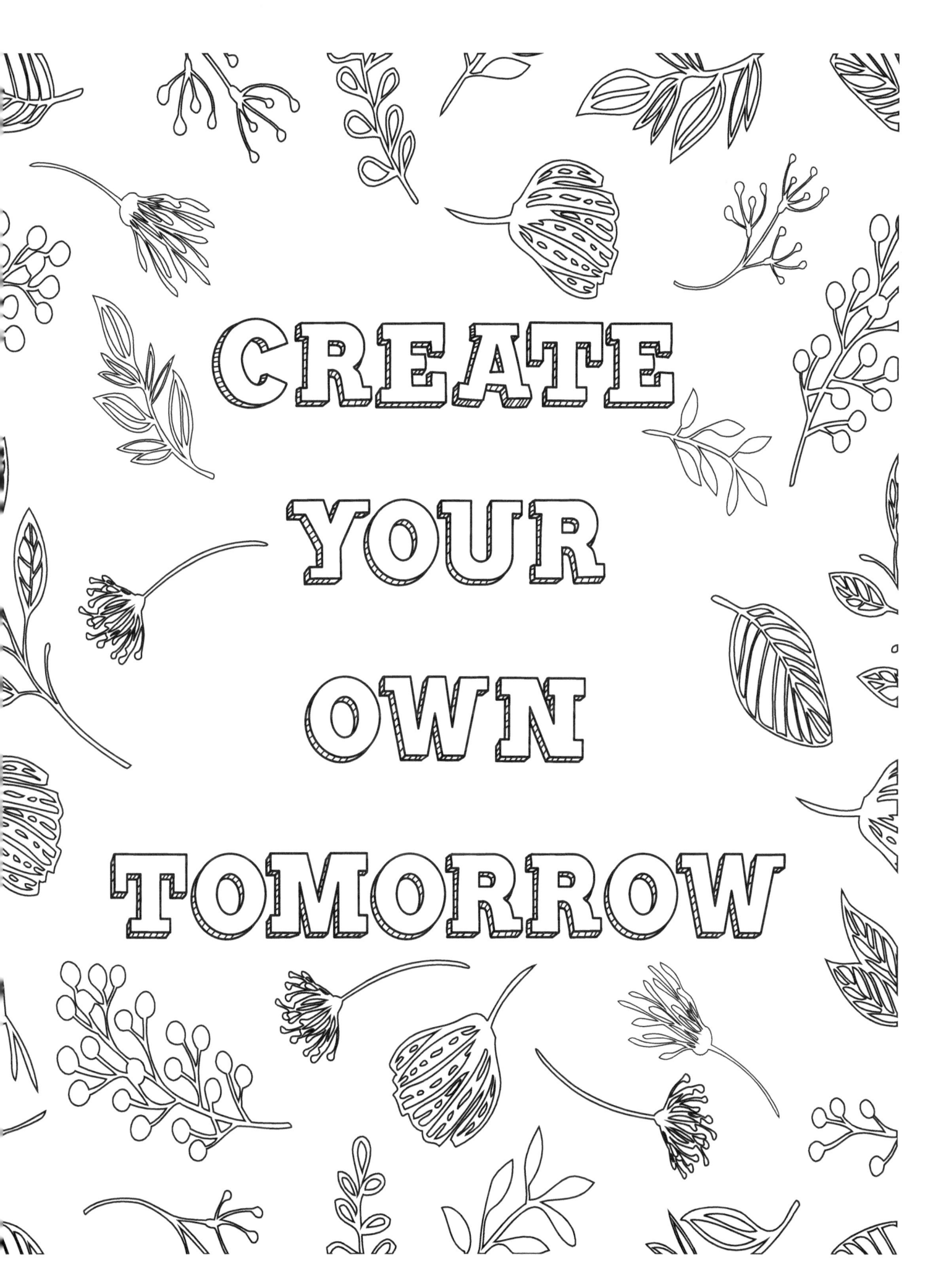

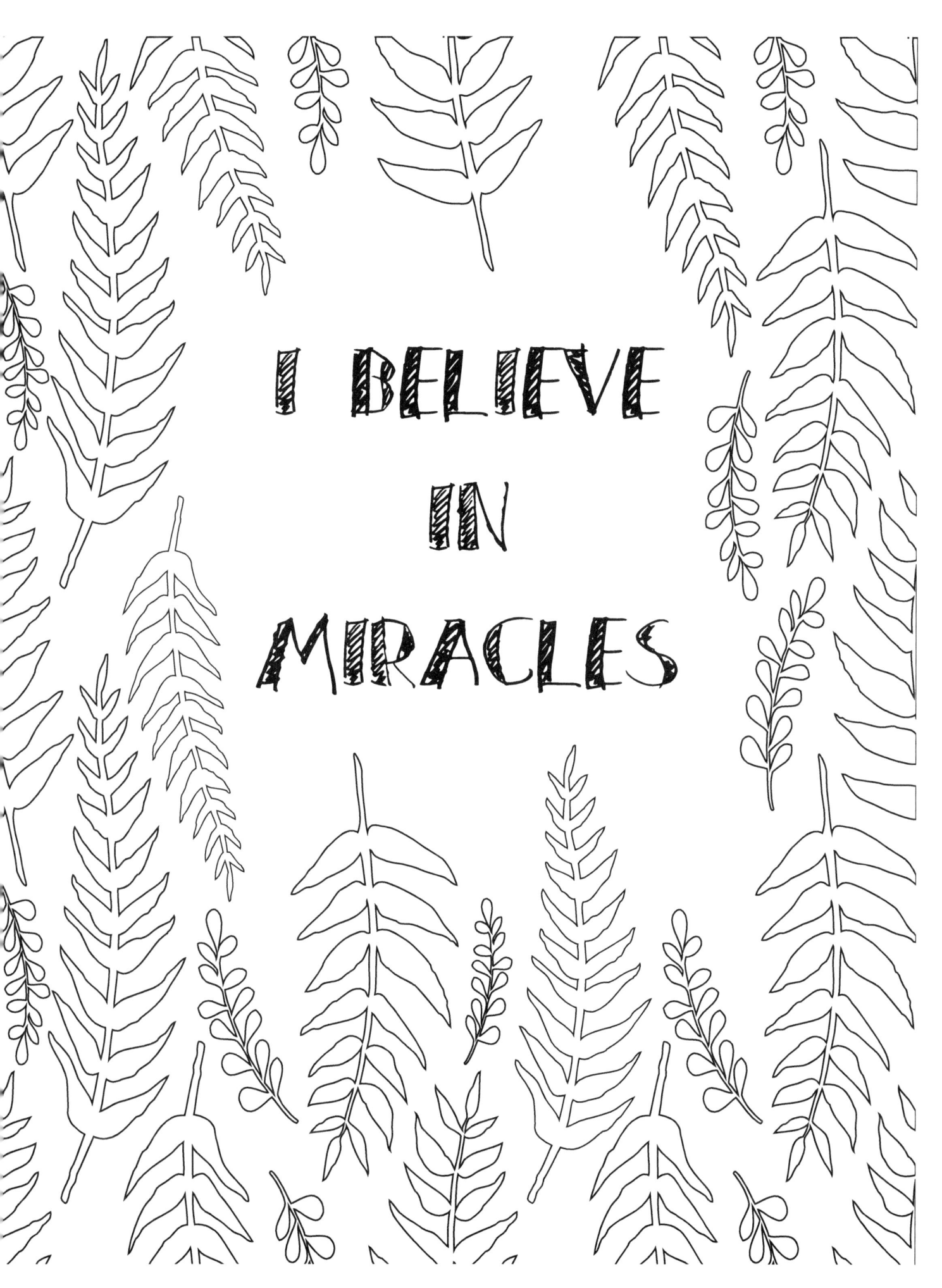

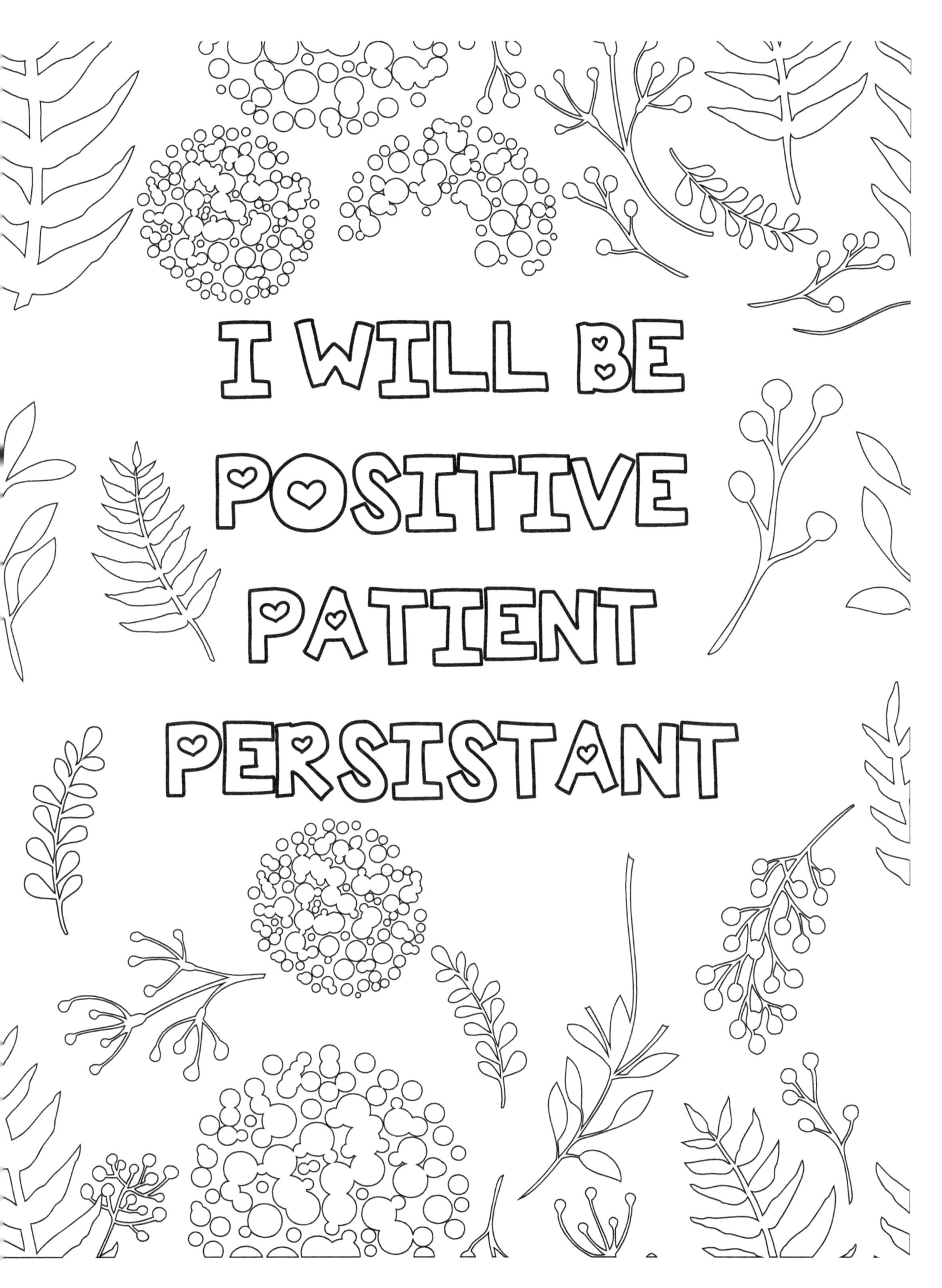

I WILL BE

POSITIVE

PATIENT

PERSISTANT

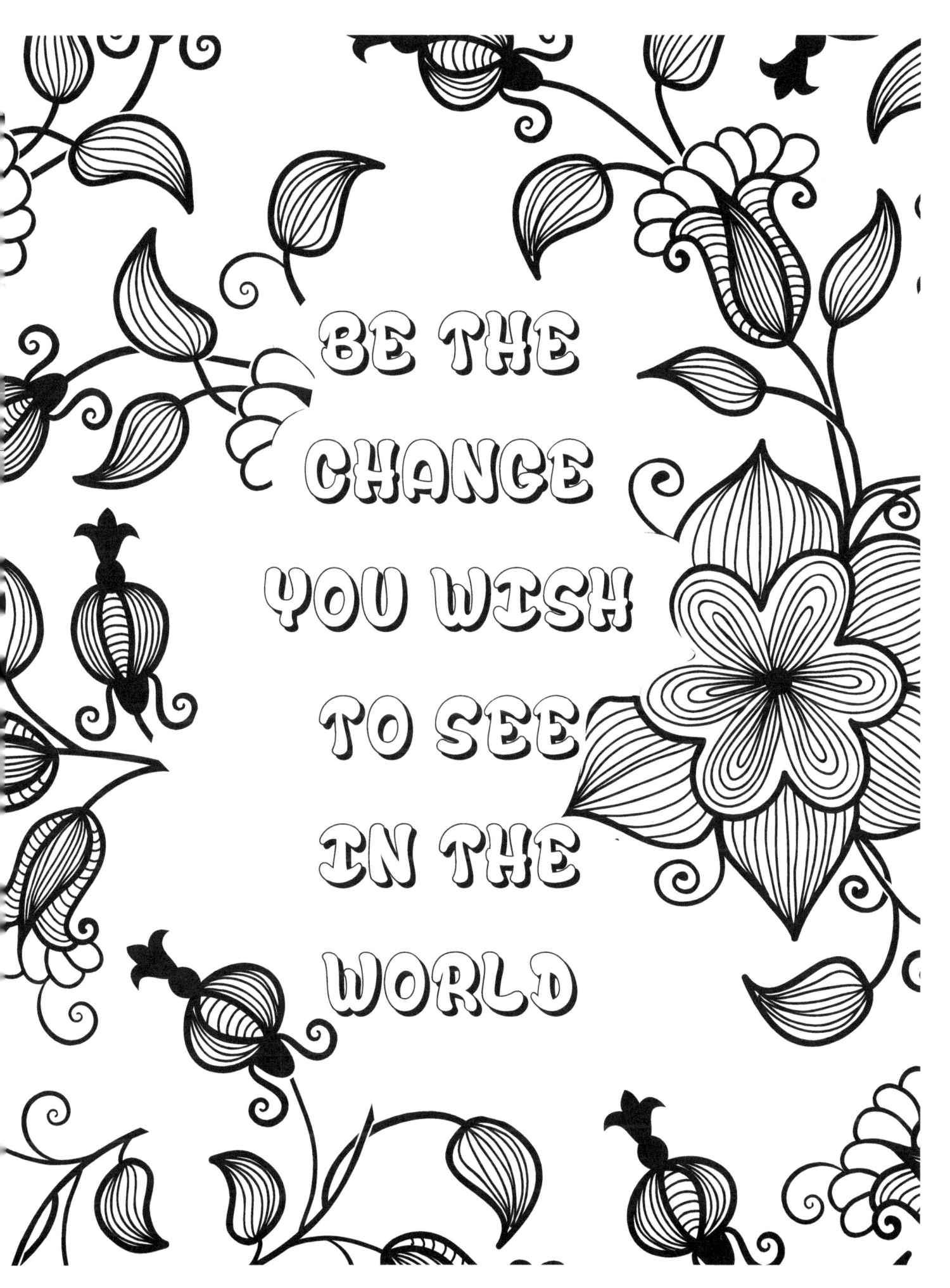

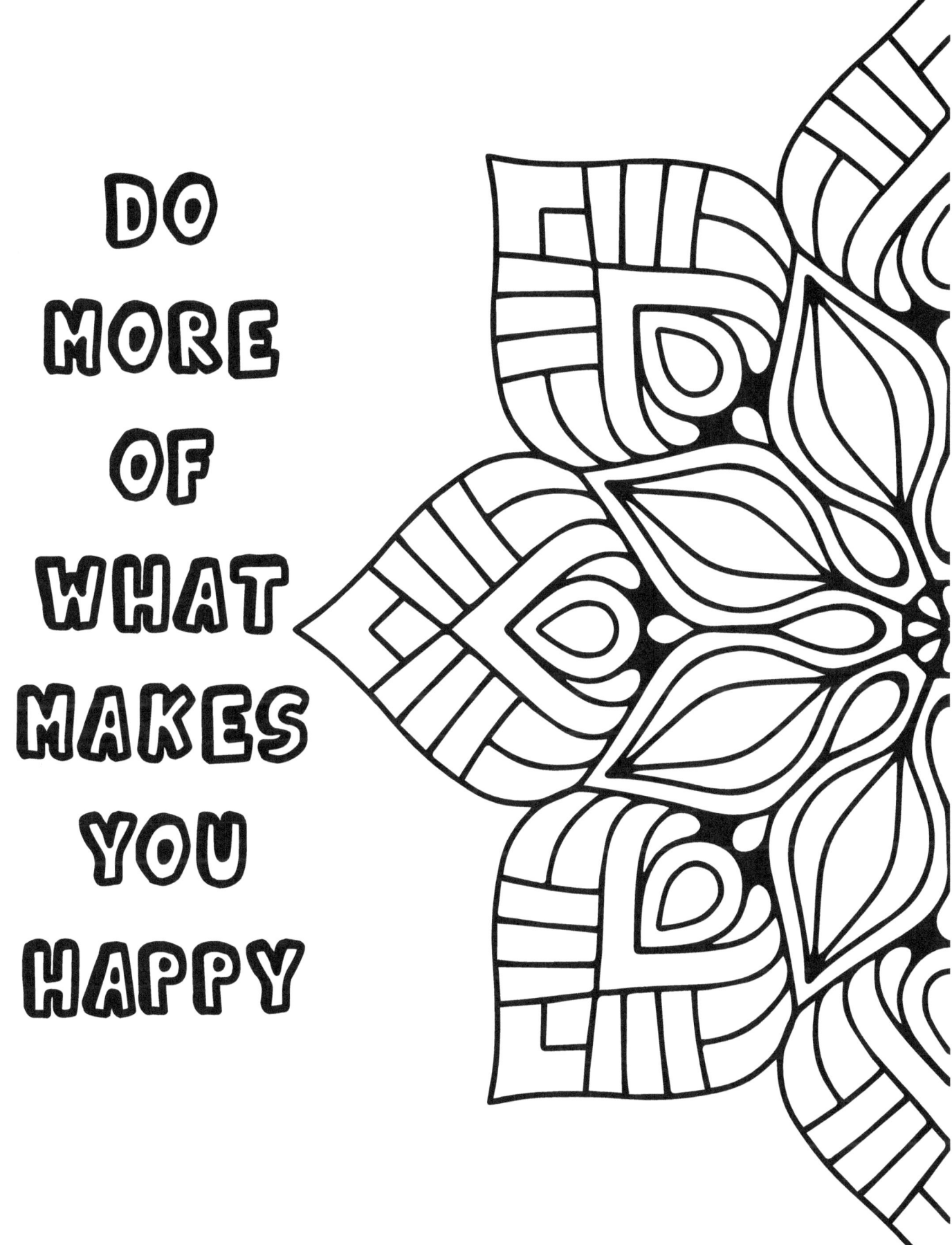

DO
MORE
OF
WHAT
MAKES
YOU
HAPPY

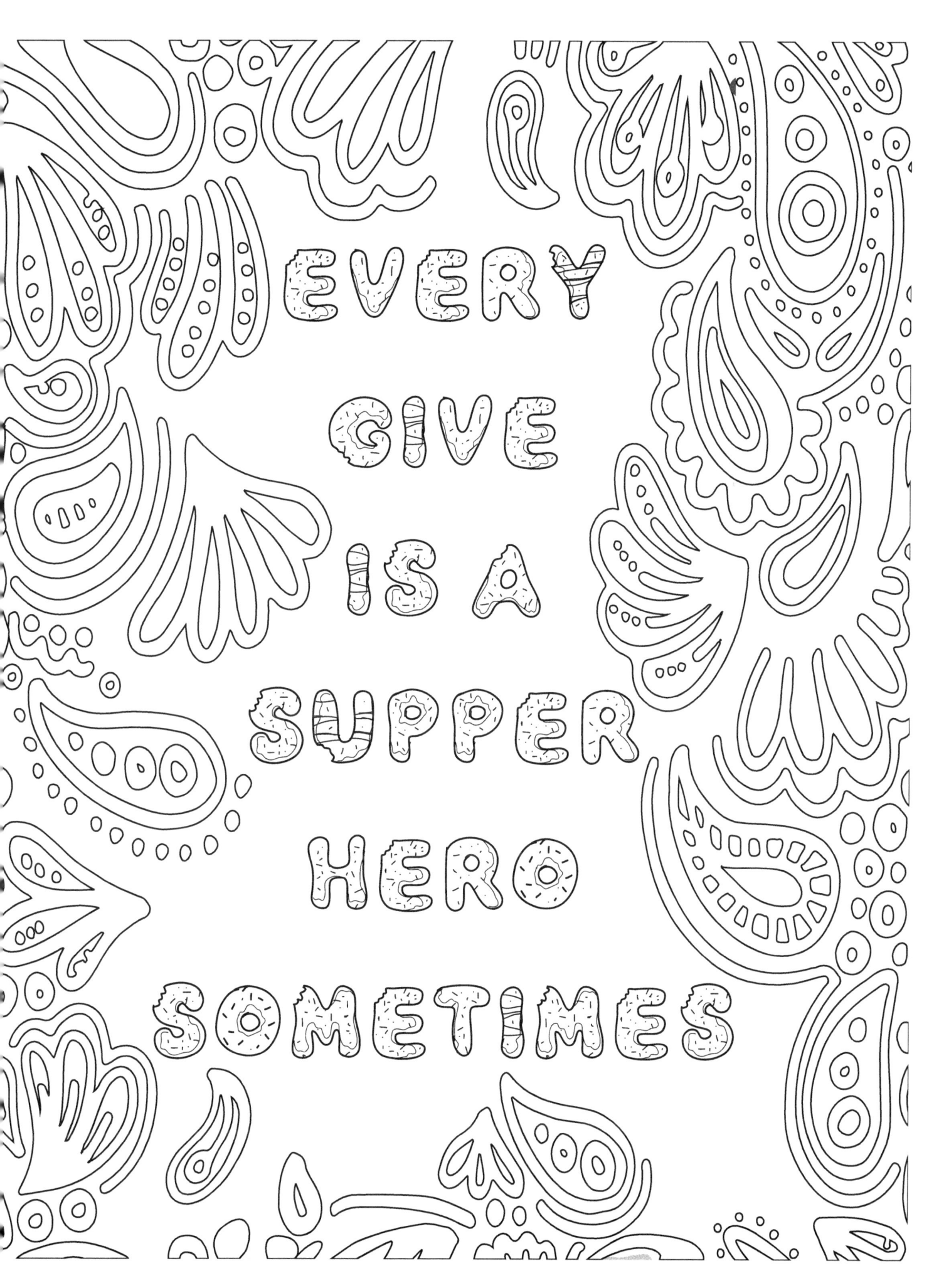

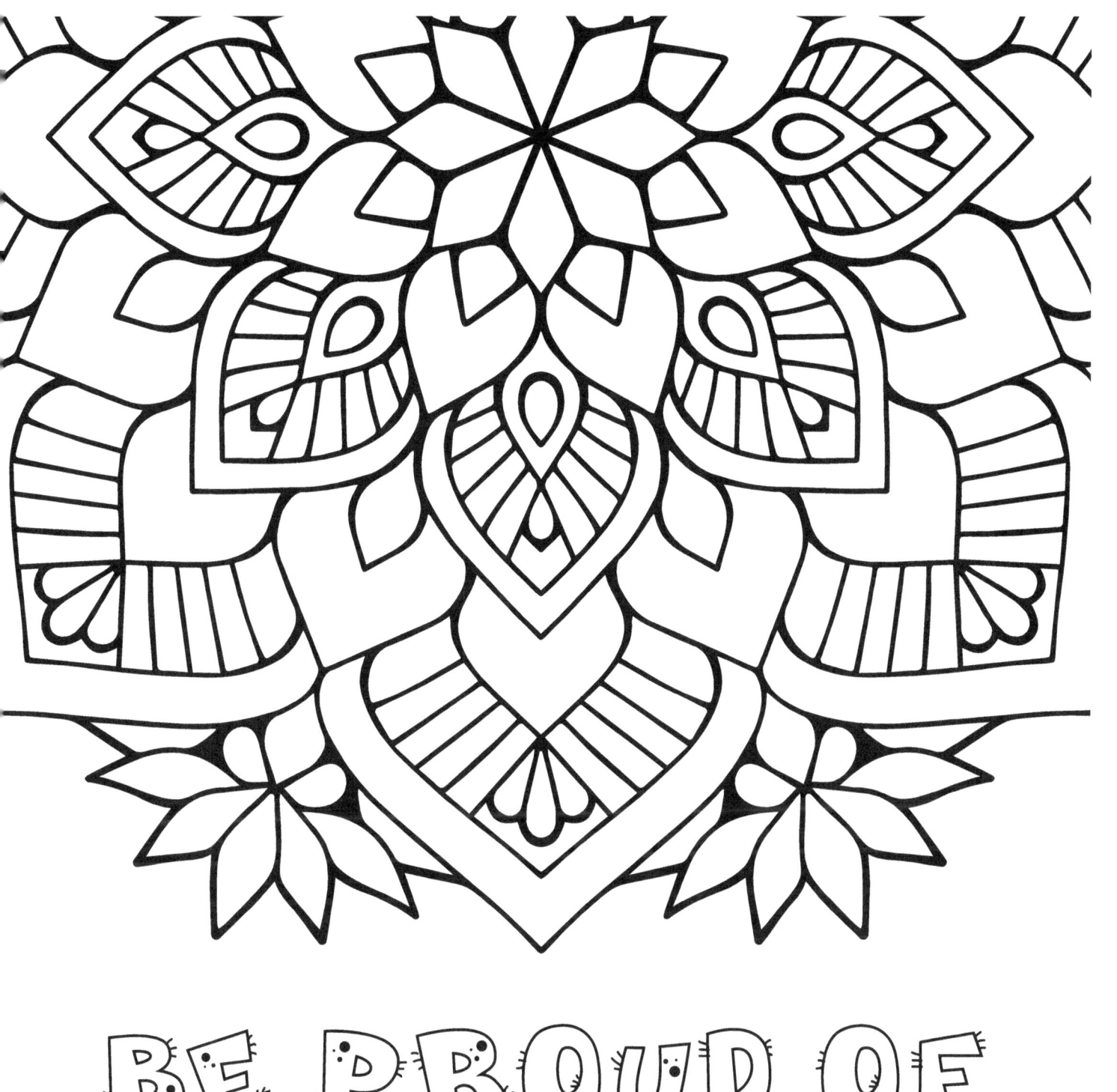

BE PROUD OF
WHO YOU ARE

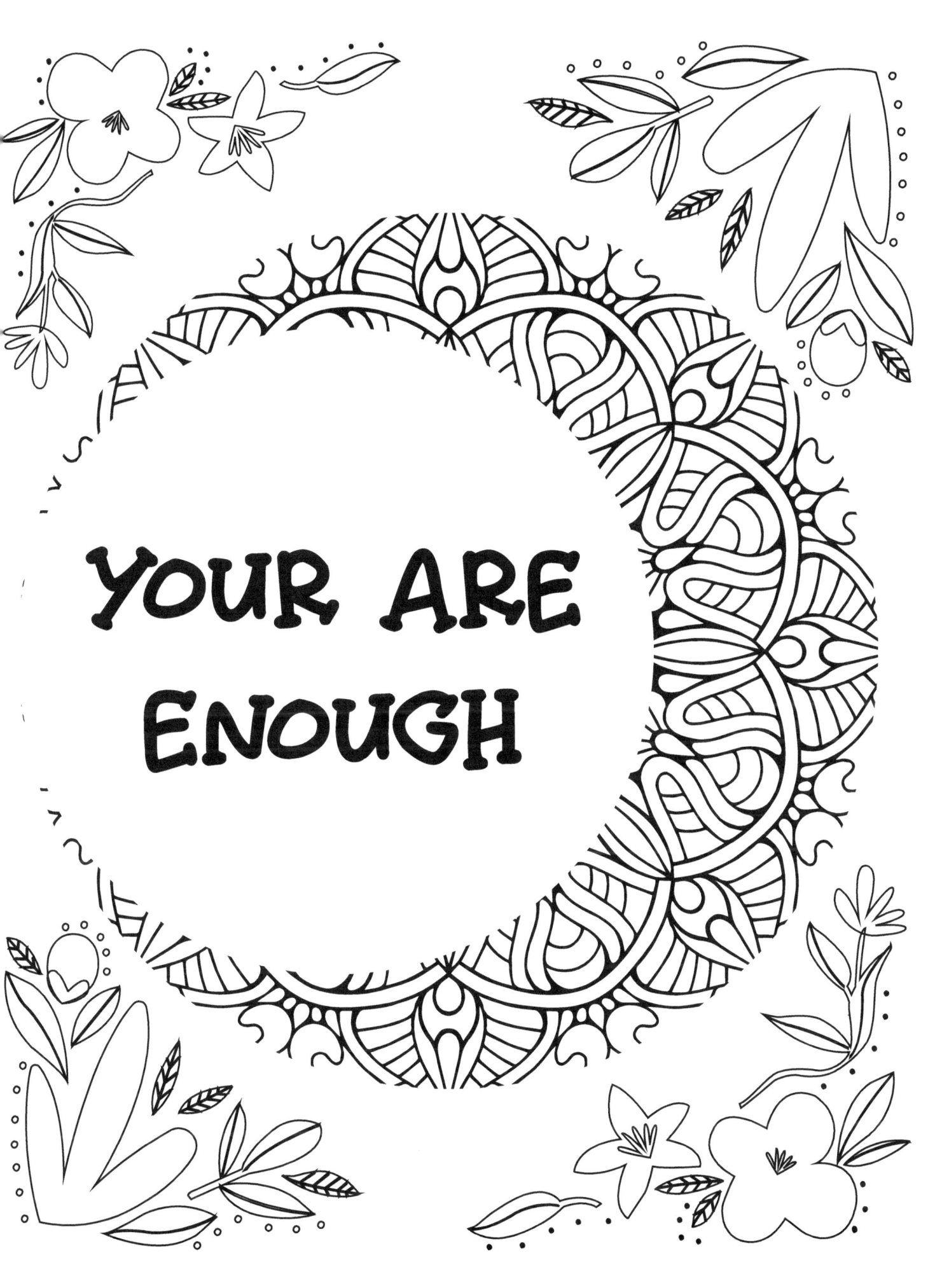

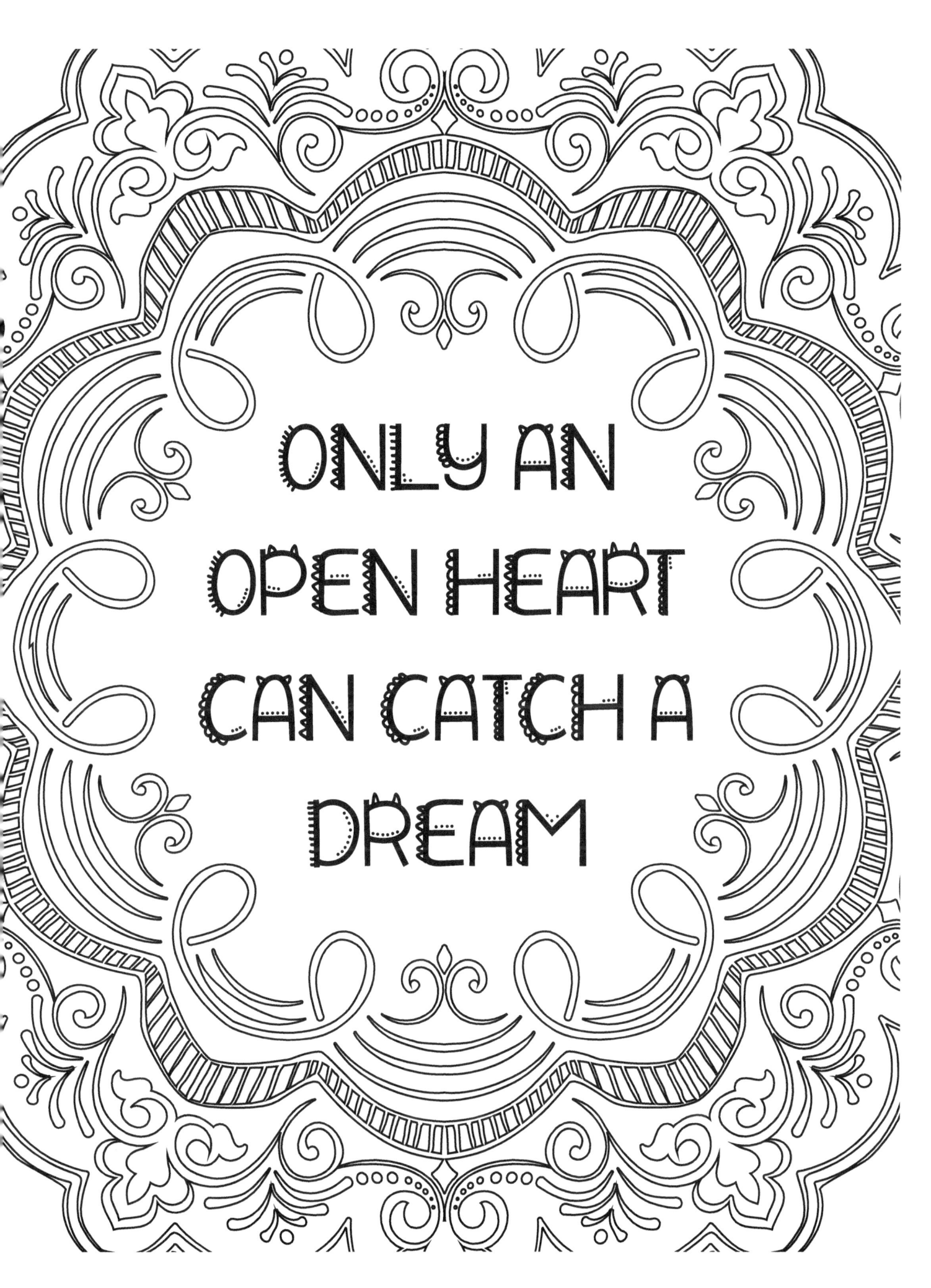

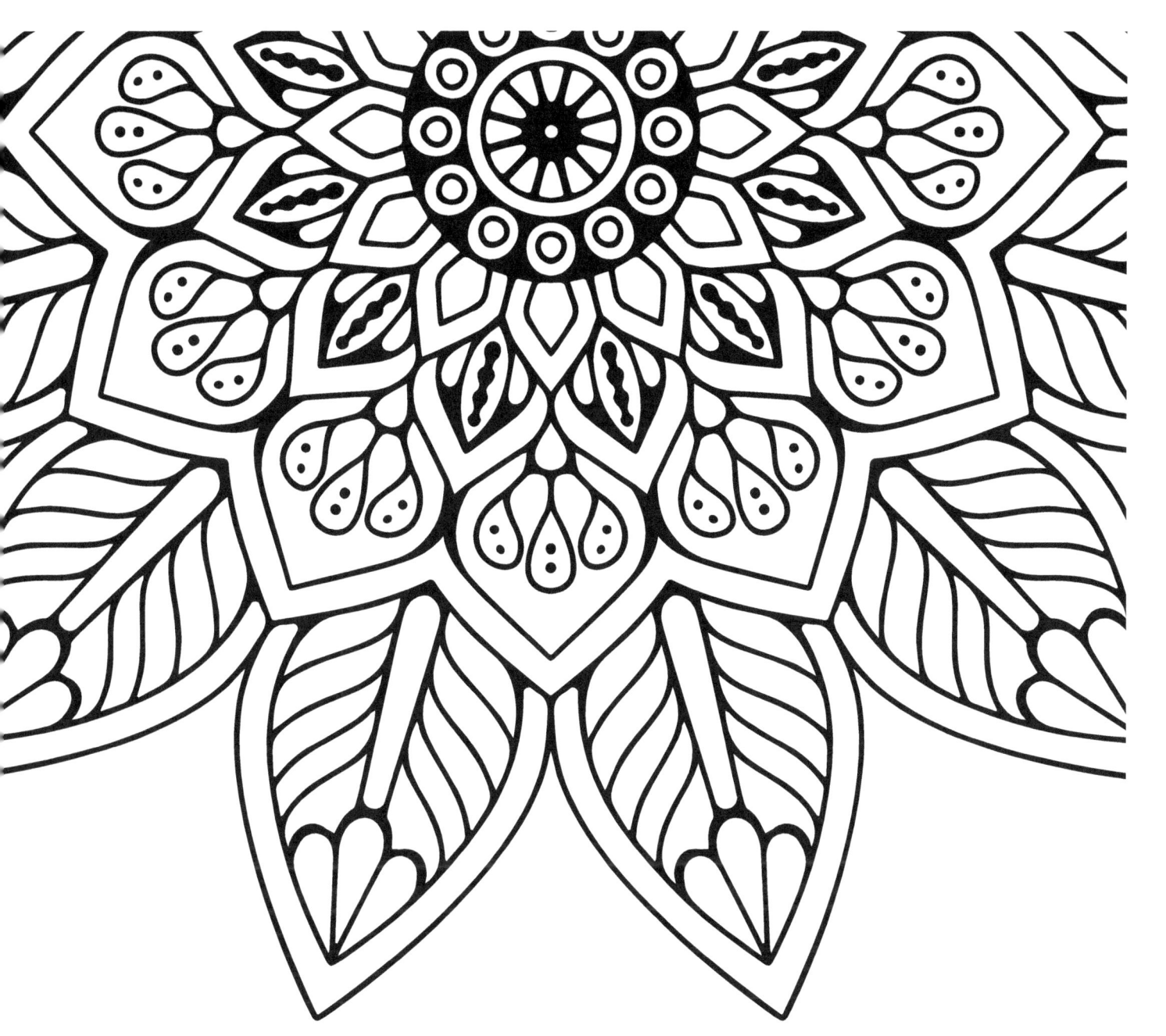

IF THERE IS NO STRUEELE THERE IS NO PROGRESS

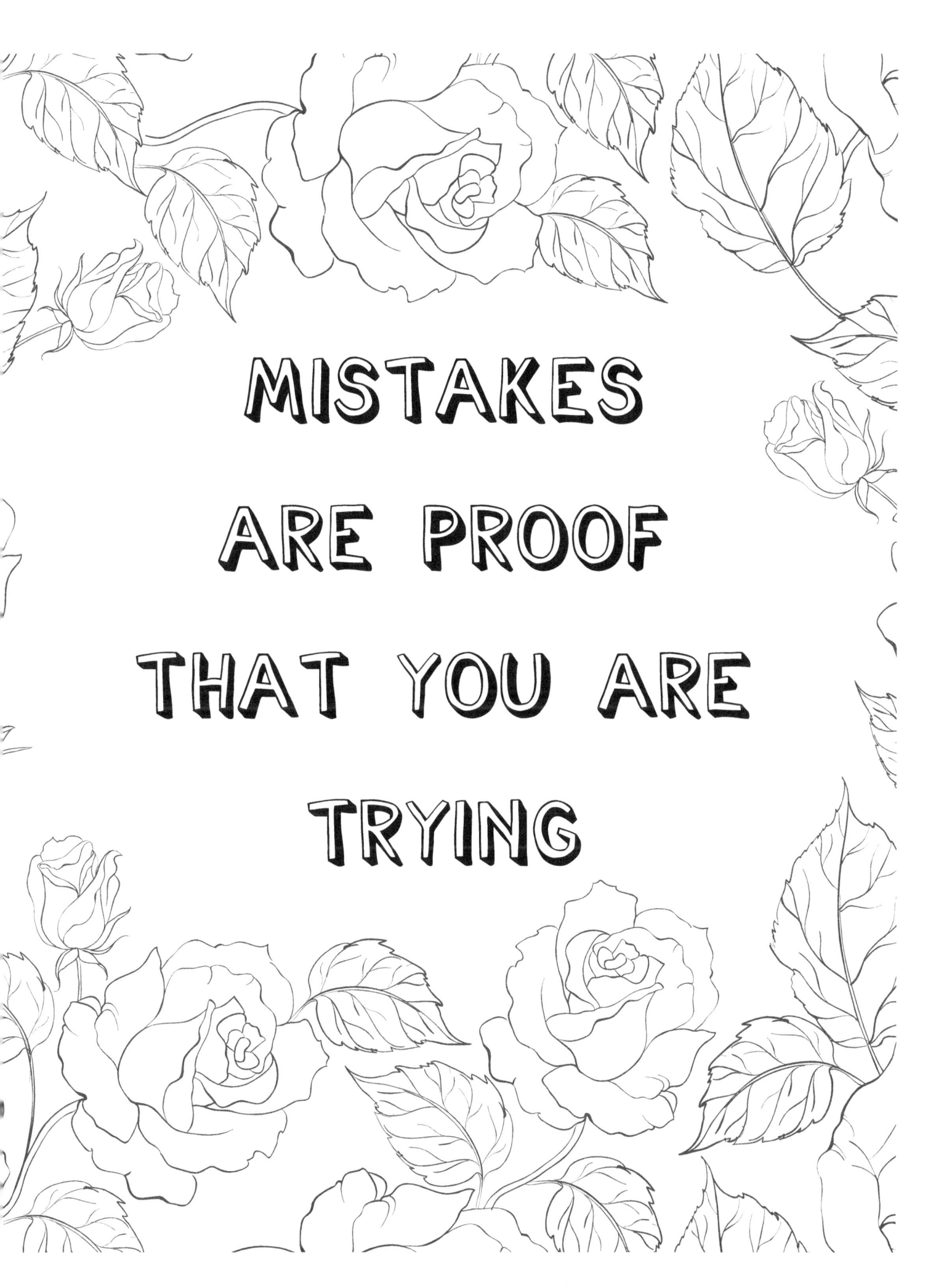

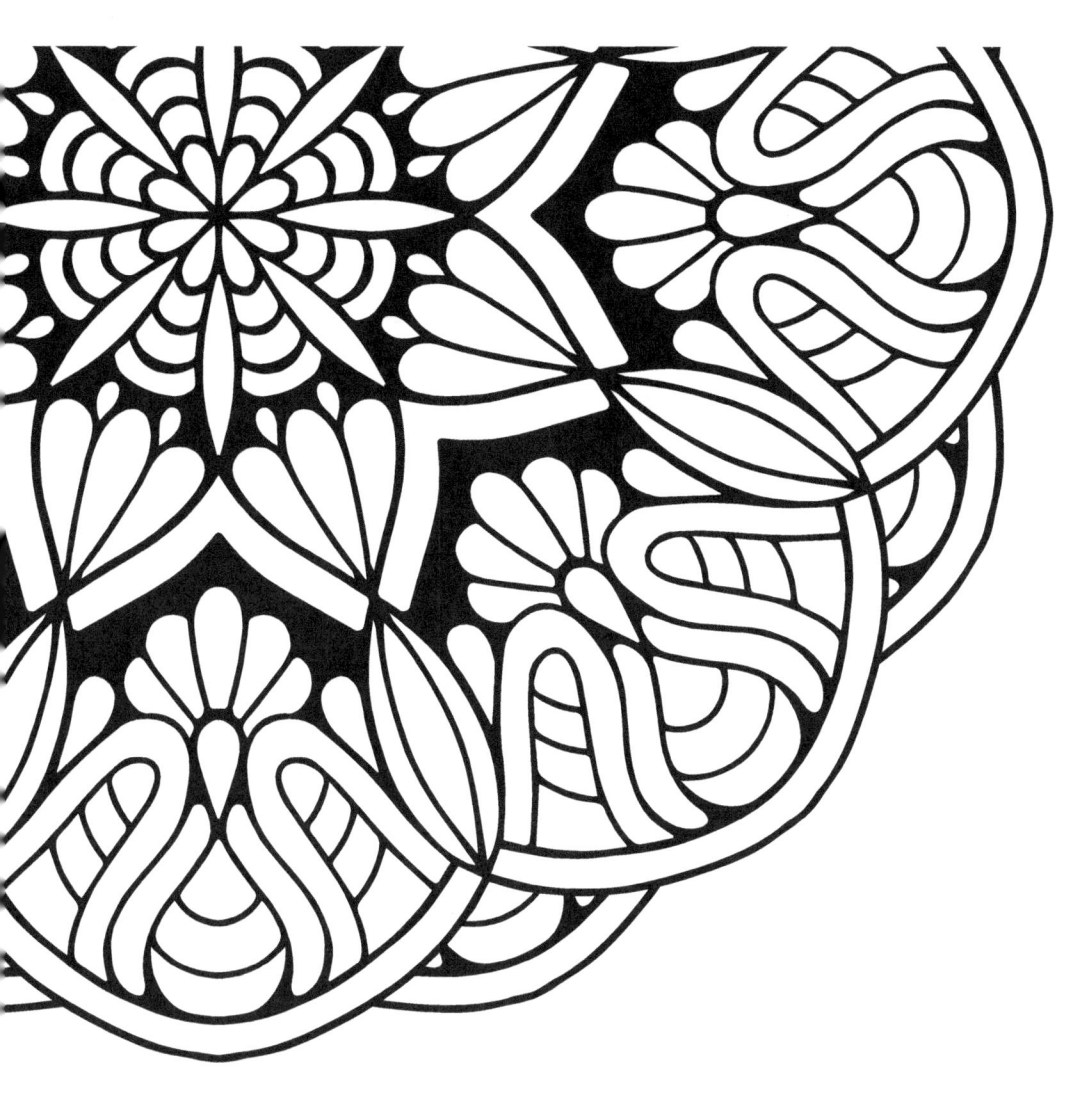

AMEZING THINGS

WILL HAPPEN TODAY

IF YOU CHOOSE

NOT TO BE

A MISERABLE COW

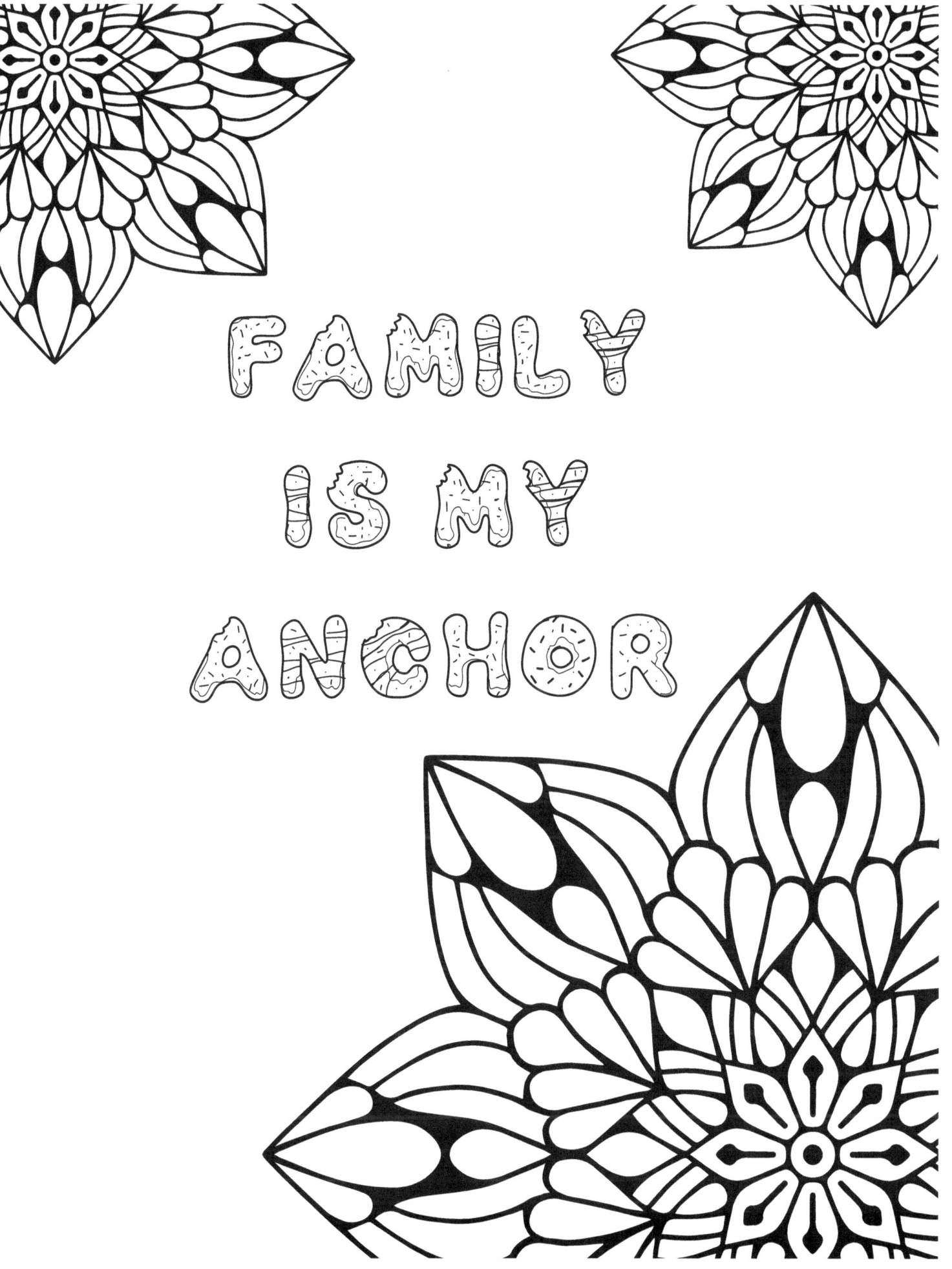

FAMILY
IS MY
ANCHOR

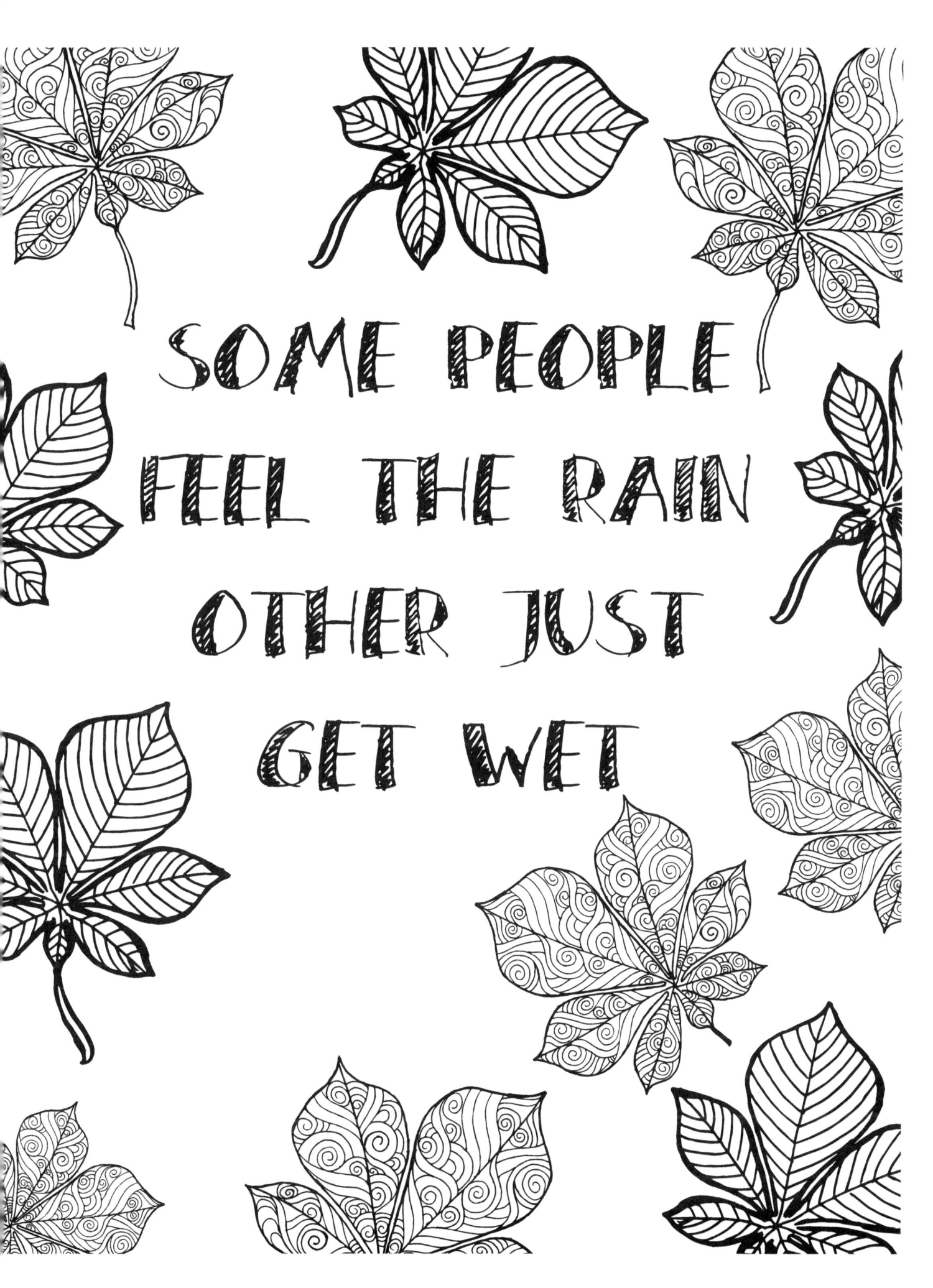

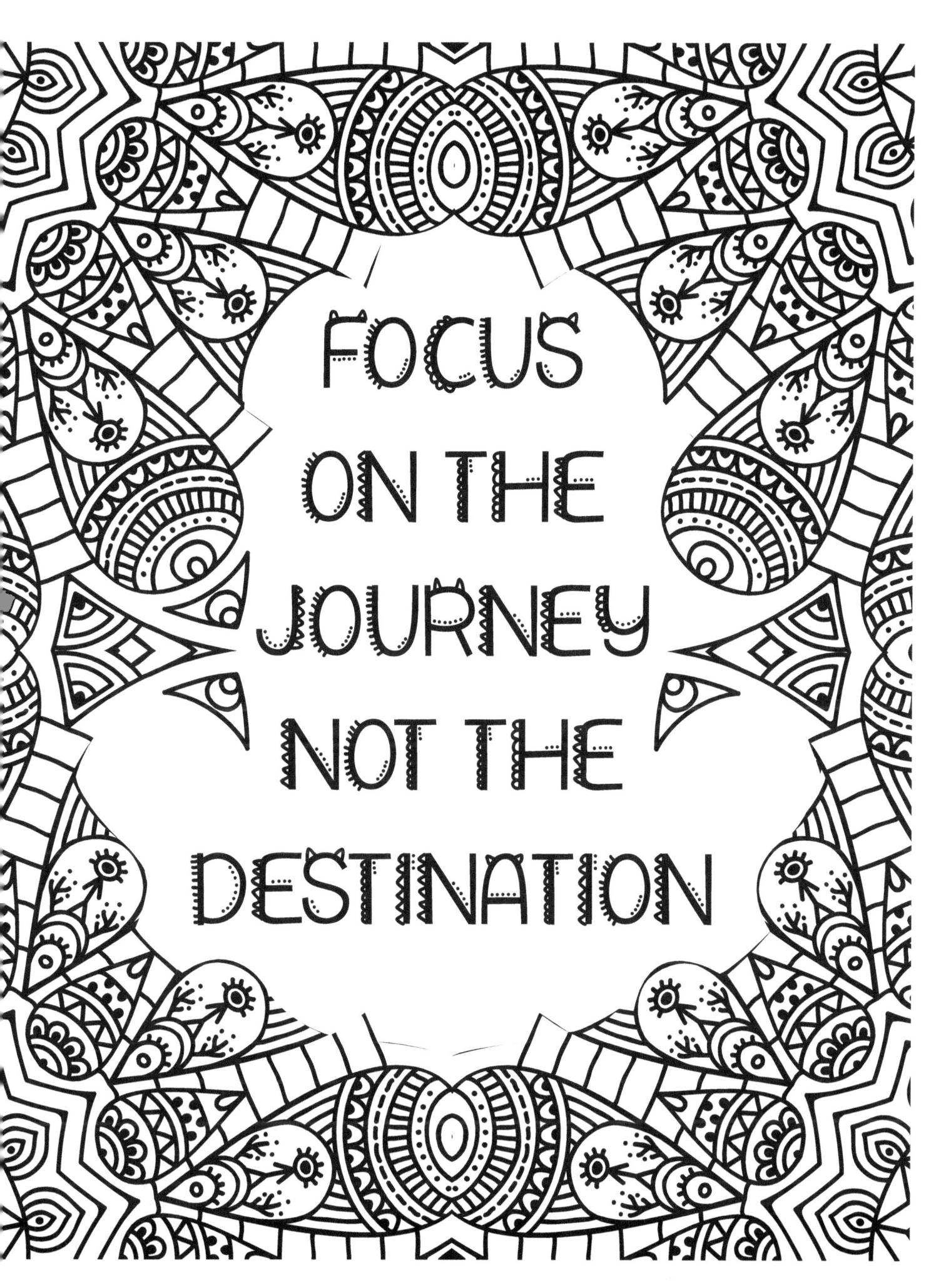

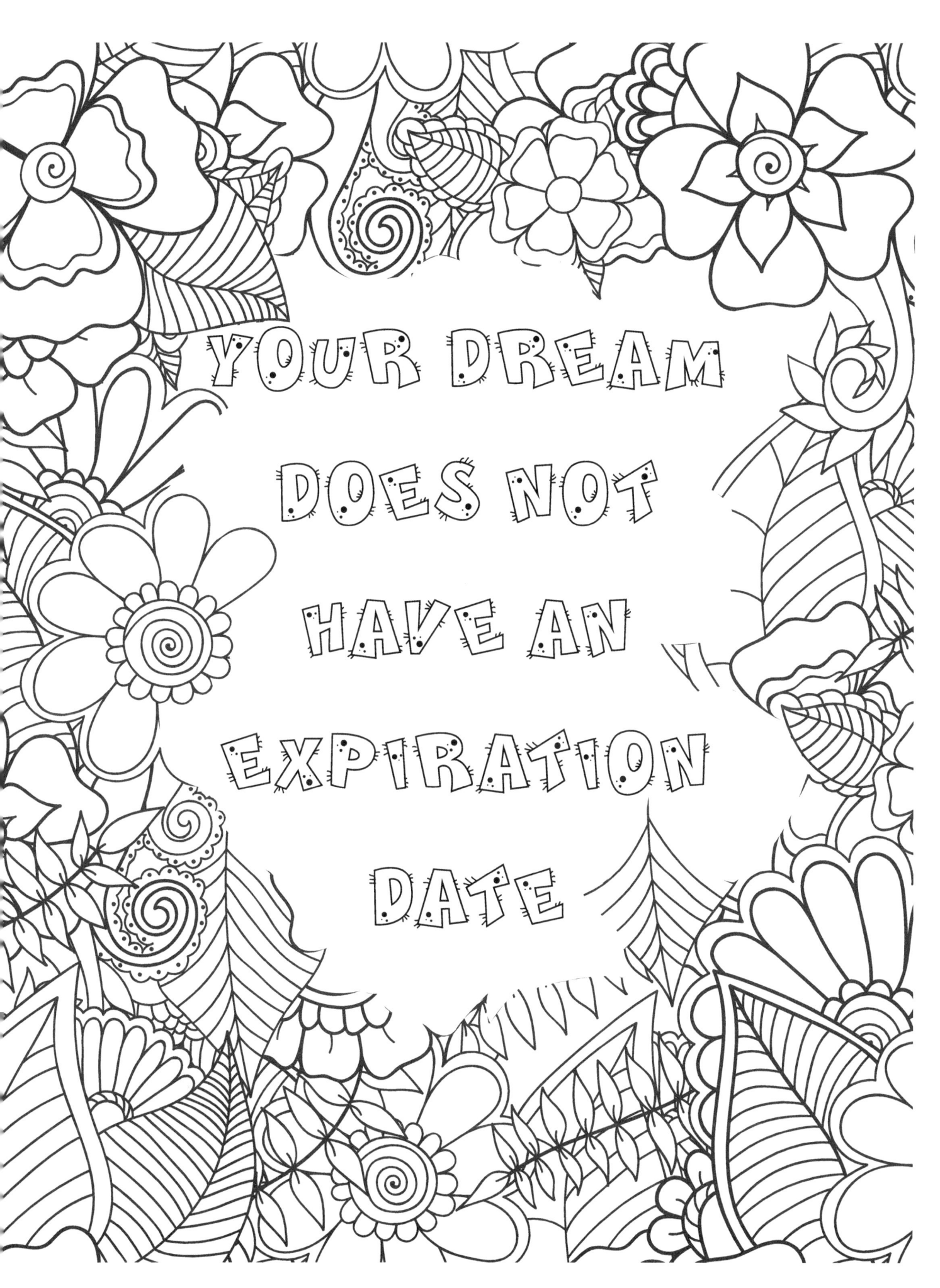

YOUR DREAM DOES NOT HAVE AN EXPIRATION DATE

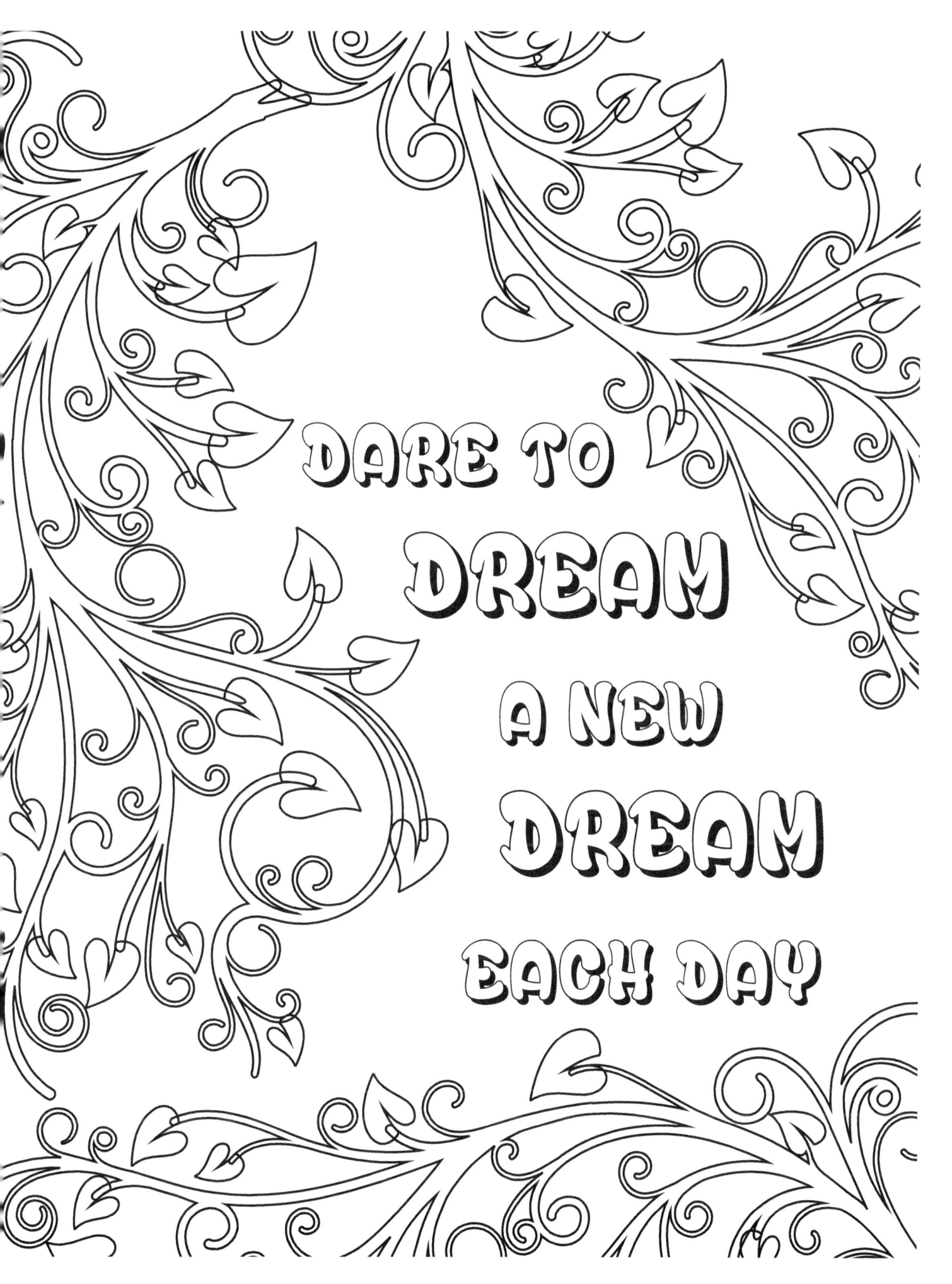

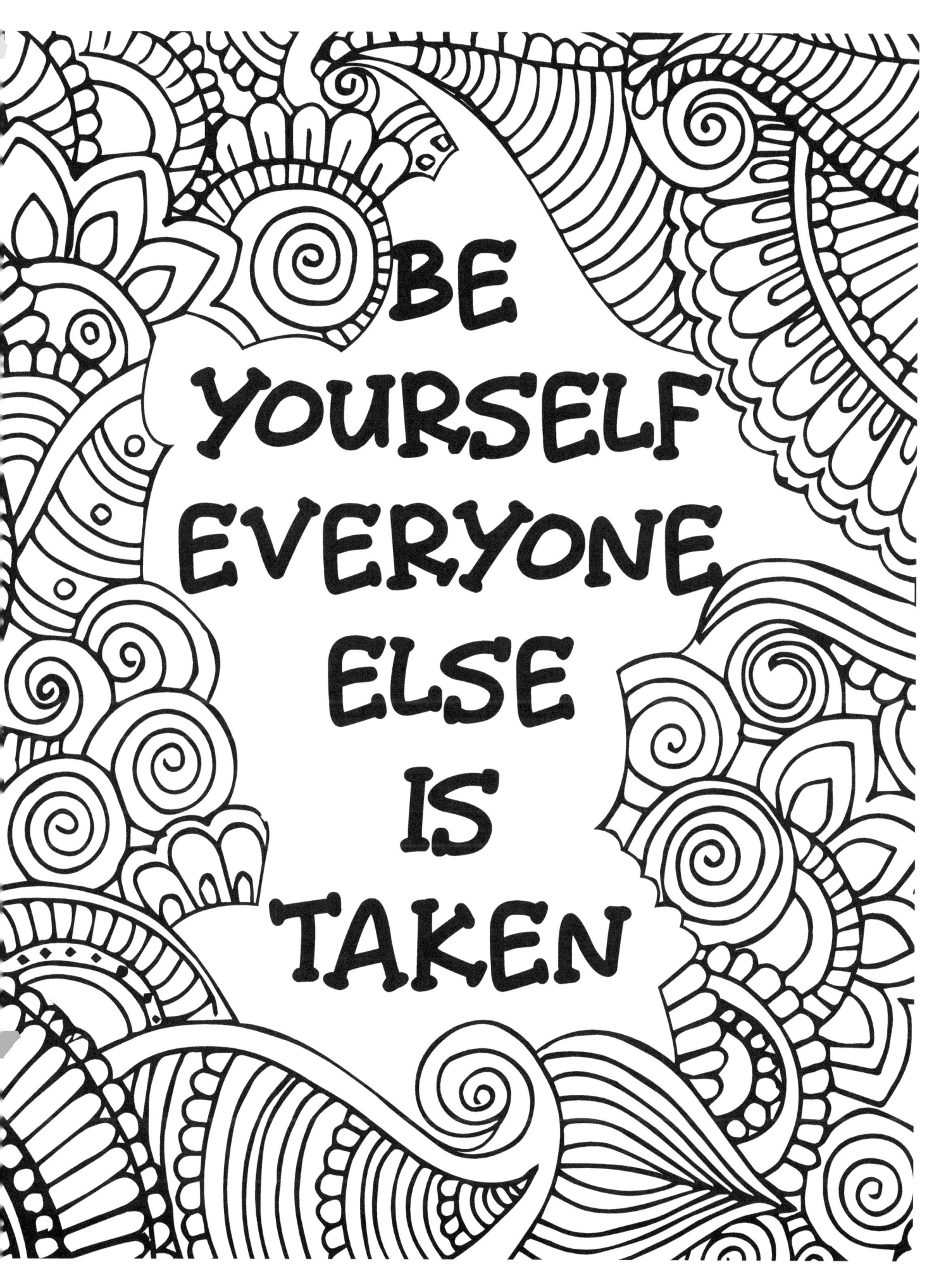

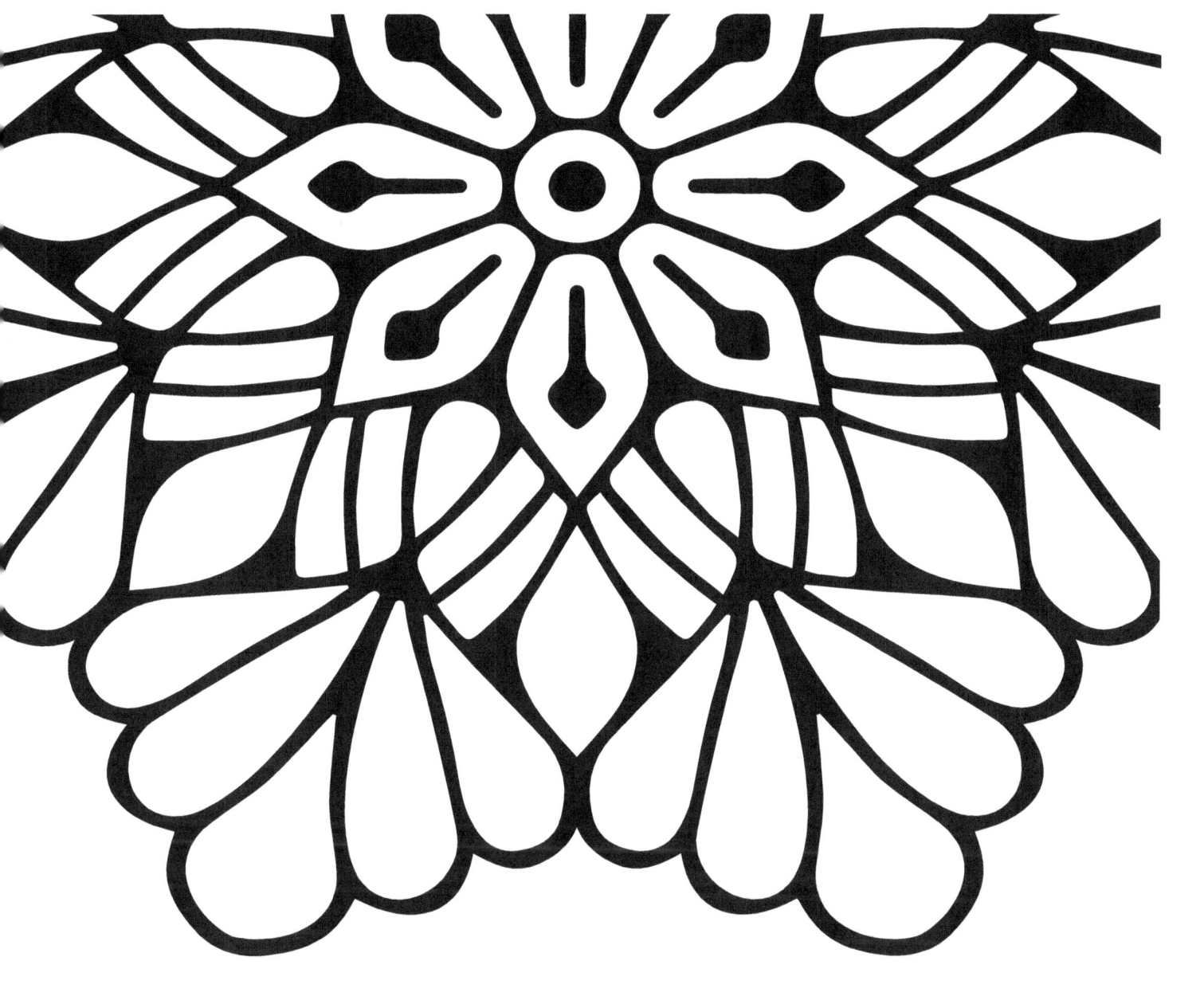

DO YOUR BEST

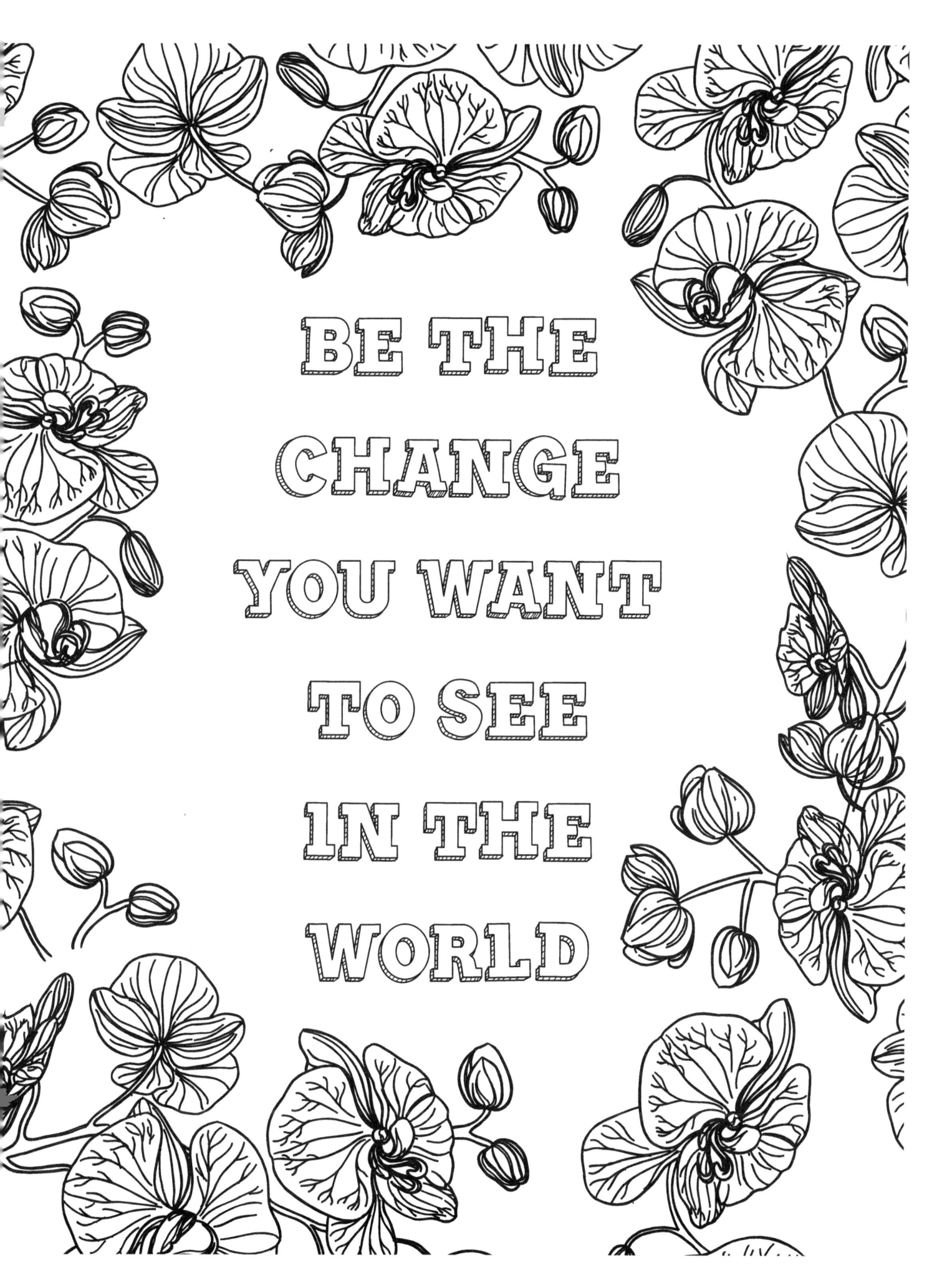

DO SOMETHING AMAZING

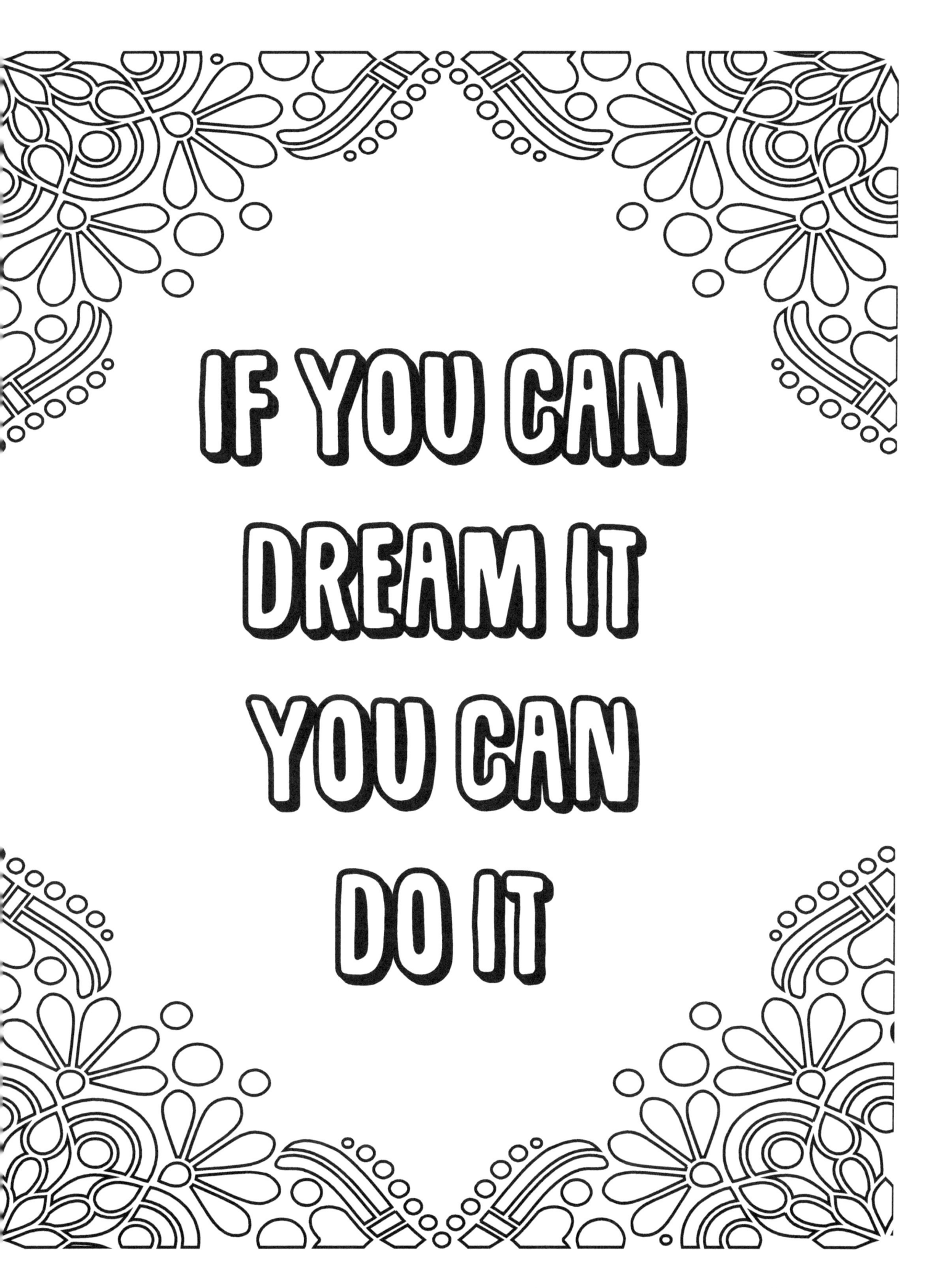

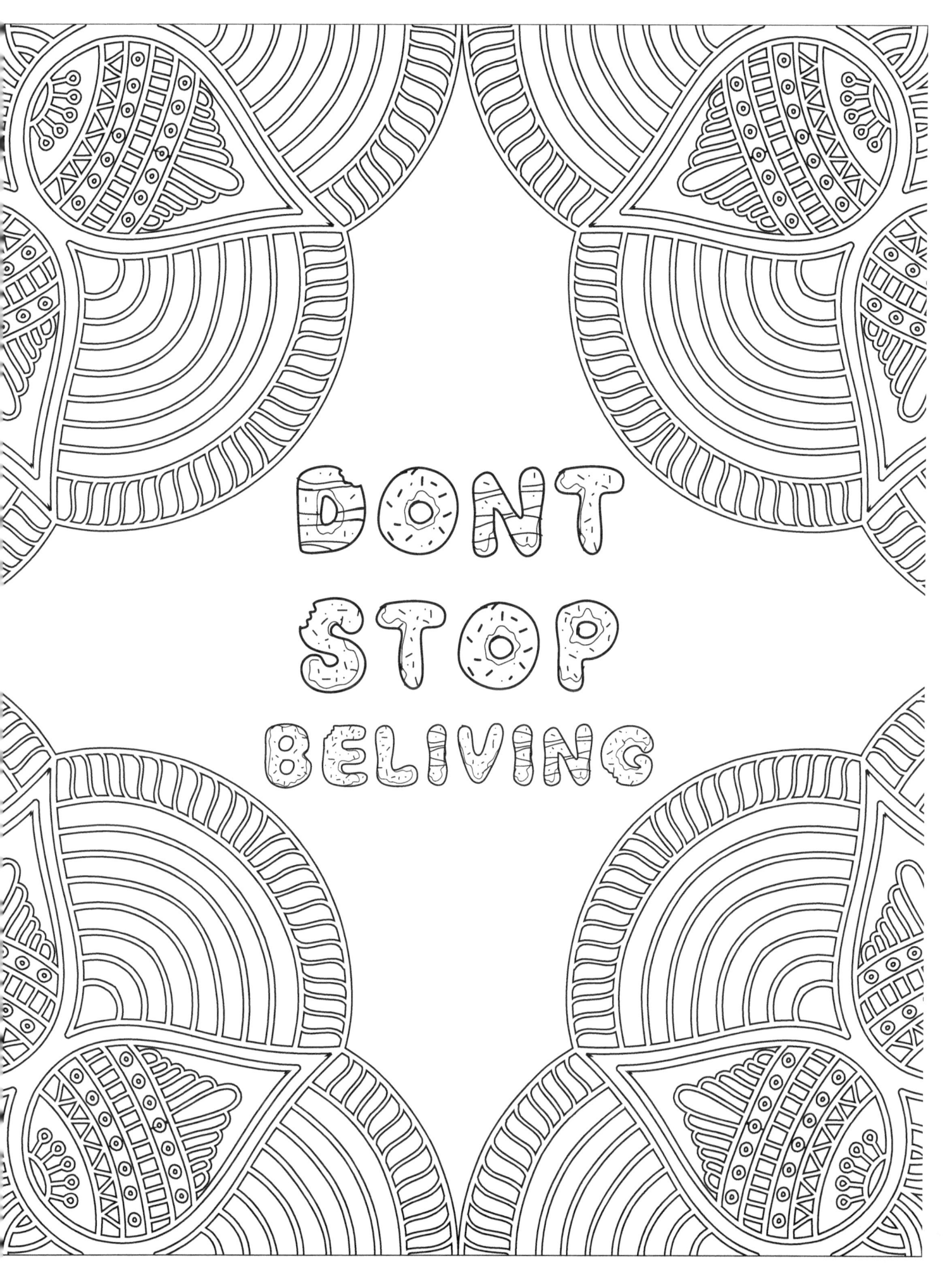